1,000,000 Books

are available to read at

www.ForgottenBooks.com

Read online
Download PDF
Purchase in print

ISBN 978-1-331-78060-1
PIBN 10233794

This book is a reproduction of an important historical work. Forgotten Books uses state-of-the-art technology to digitally reconstruct the work, preserving the original format whilst repairing imperfections present in the aged copy. In rare cases, an imperfection in the original, such as a blemish or missing page, may be replicated in our edition. We do, however, repair the vast majority of imperfections successfully; any imperfections that remain are intentionally left to preserve the state of such historical works.

Forgotten Books is a registered trademark of FB &c Ltd.
Copyright © 2018 FB &c Ltd.
FB &c Ltd, Dalton House, 60 Windsor Avenue, London, SW19 2RR.
Company number 08720141. Registered in England and Wales.

For support please visit www.forgottenbooks.com

1 MONTH OF FREE READING

at

www.ForgottenBooks.com

By purchasing this book you are eligible for one month membership to ForgottenBooks.com, giving you unlimited access to our entire collection of over 1,000,000 titles via our web site and mobile apps.

To claim your free month visit:

www.forgottenbooks.com/free233794

* Offer is valid for 45 days from date of purchase. Terms and conditions apply.

English
Français
Deutsche
Italiano
Español
Português

www.forgottenbooks.com

Mythology Photography **Fiction** Fishing Christianity **Art** Cooking Essays Buddhism Freemasonry Medicine **Biology** Music **Ancient Egypt** Evolution Carpentry Physics Dance Geology **Mathematics** Fitness Shakespeare **Folklore** Yoga Marketing **Confidence** Immortality Biographies Poetry **Psychology** Witchcraft Electronics Chemistry History **Law** Accounting **Philosophy** Anthropology Alchemy Drama Quantum Mechanics Atheism Sexual Health **Ancient History Entrepreneurship** Languages Sport Paleontology Needlework Islam **Metaphysics** Investment Archaeology Parenting Statistics Criminology **Motivational**

OF

ROMANCE AND CHIVALRY.

BY

W. STEWART ROSS.

LONDON:
W. STEWART & CO., THE HOLBORN VIADUCT STEPS, E.C.
EDINBURGH: J. MENZIES & CO.

*Morrison and Gibb, Edinburgh,
Printers to Her Majesty's Stationery Office.*

CONTENTS.

	PAGE
ROMAN PERIOD—	
Caractacus the Briton,	1
Graeme,	4
Eric Haaerfager,	14
Raid of the Vikingr,	20
The Minstrel King,	22
Edith,	25
Hereward,	26
The Ampulla,	30
Richard Lion-Heart,	34
The Ringlet of Lenore,	37
The Red-Cross Knight,	41
The Pale Bride,	45
The Death of Wallace,	46
Death of Edward the First,	48
Elinore,	51
The Bride of Steel,	54
Never more,	56
The Choice of Sigismund,	58
Glencoe,	63
Culloden,	66
Chivalry,	70
L'Envoi,	74

LAYS OF ROMANCE AND CHIVALRY.

CARACTACUS THE BRITON.

Adown the Via Sacra,[1]
  In the noonday's golden glow,
Rolled the thunder of the Triumph,
  Two thousand years ago.

And through the crowded Forum
  Passed the triumphal car;
And o'er the shouting thousands
  Waved the standards of the war.

Blazing with gold and green with palms,
  On moved the mighty show;—
Above, proud Roman eagles,[2]
  Stout Roman hearts below.

Ho! Vict'ry's crown of laurel!
  Ho! Victor's ruddy wine!
Ho! branches from the terraces
  Of woody Aventine![3]

---

[1] *Via Sacra*, the 'Sacred Way.' The *Triumph*, a grand procession in honour of a victorious Roman general, passed along the *Via Sacra*, through the *Forum* or market-place (where the law courts also were), and up to the *Capitol*, where a white bull was sacrificed to Jupiter.

[2] The eagle, the wolf, the horse, and the boar were the standards of the Roman legion, but the *eagle* was the most general.

[3] One of the seven hills on which Rome was built.

And the thunder of the shouting
    Pealed through the sultry air,
And sword and spear were brandished
    By right arms strong and bare;[1]—

The arms that hewed out glory
    Through many a bloody day,—
The arms that bore Rome's eagle
    From Ganges to the Tay.

'To plant that Roman eagle
    On Cambrian[2] battle-field,
Aid, Mars! red god of battle!
    Ostorius'[3] sword and shield!

'Shout for the great Ostorius,
    Far o'er the ocean foam!
Shout for him, yellow Tiber!
    Shout, Seven Hills of Rome!'

Still is the triumph moving,
    The eagles wave in air;
Flash a hundred thousand weapons,
    A thousand trumpets blare.

But, toiling to Jove's temple,
    With weary steps and slow,
The haggard prisoners totter,
    In suffering and woe.

---

[1] In the ordinary panoply the arms of the soldiery were left unprotected.

[2] *Cambria*, the ancient name for Wales, where the Britons made their last and most desperate stand.

[3] *Ostorius Scapula*, the Roman general who defeated and captured Caractacus, and who for this was honoured with the triumph referred to in the poem

Hair matted, and eyes streaming,
    They march on four-and-four;[1]
Their wounds are raw and ghastly,
    And stiff with dust and gore.

Won were those deep wounds bravely
    In Britain's far-off isle,
Stemming the Roman legions
    In Plynlimmon's red defile!

And Rome, with all her valour,
    Toiled till the set of sun,
And grappled ankle-deep in blood,
    Ere that defile was won!

Now she insults the fallen—
    Who march on four-and-four,
Chains clanking and mien haggard,
    Wounds stiff with dust and gore.

The hindmost of the captives,
    A king serene and high,
Marches erect and fearless,
    Wild daring in his eye!

What brow like his to wear a crown!
    What hand to wield the glaive!—
Caractacus the Briton,
    The bravest of the brave!

Heed not, O gallant soldier!
    A deathless name is thine,
When power has left Mount Cœlius[2]
    And ruined Aventine;—

---

[1] The prisoners taken in war, along with the spoils of captured cities, preceded the triumphal car.
[2] Mount Cœlius, another of the seven hills.

When History scarce remembers
   The grandeur now before thee,
She'll blazon on her brightest page
   The far-off isle that bore thee.

And when the world recalleth
   Time's misty yesterday,
She'll offer thee, Caractacus,
   The laurel and the lay.

Two thousand years of story
   Now part this age from thine,
And many a deed of glory
   Has graced thy land and mine;

Yet, brilliant in the muster
   Of the deathless in the grave,
Shines CARACTACUS THE BRITON,
   The bravest of the brave!

GRAEME.

FAR back in forgotten ages,
   'Mong the misty years of time,
Was enacted, lords and ladies,
   This the subject of my rhyme.

Long ago when fierce Selgovae,
   Naked, battled with the gale,
Lived a lovely Druid maiden
   In the wilds of Niddesdale.

And far, far was her father famed
   Among our hero sires of yore;

A braver ne'er war-chariot manned,
　　A stronger arm ne'er target bore.

And ponderous hung his iron sword,
　　Without a scabbard, at his thigh;
Flashed in the might of manhood's bloom
　　The azure of his martial eye.

All plaited round his warrior brow,
　　His auburn hair a helmet made,
That might withstand 'mid battle's toil
　　The downward swing of iron blade.

Yet graceful o'er his necklace fell
　　Luxuriant tresses wet with dew,
That aye, as sighed the morning breeze,
　　Light o'er his powerful shoulders flew.

His necklace hung down o'er his breast,
　　Gleaming with shells and burning gold;
And hung loose o'er his manly form
　　His deerskin mantle's graceful fold.

In sooth he was a gallant chief—
　　The Druid minstrels sang his fame;
There was not grove nor fort but knew
　　The prowess of the fearless Graeme.

Brightly dawned a summer morn
　　O'er yellow wastes of whins and broom,
O'er hoary cairns and lonely moors,
　　Empurpled with the heather bloom.

O'er cromlechs rocking in the wind,
　　On distant hill-sides drear and grey,
And on the ocean-leaguered rocks,
　　Fell the red light of dawning day.

Jocund rose that day of yore—
    The painted hunter grasped his spear;
The wild-wood echoed bay and shout,
    And sprang agile the hunted deer.

And foremost in the chase was Graeme,
    Who wrought his foemen such annoy;
Right noble seemed that warrior proud—
    The gallant Graeme—the Druid's joy!

See at his heels his savage horde,
    'Mong morning's mist fantastic curl'd;
They're bursting through the trackless wild,
    These warriors of a former world.

And pressing forward in the van,
    Of lovely mien and deadly aim,
'Tis she upon that fiery steed—
    The daughter of the fearless Graeme.

'Tis she, the peerless Druid maid,
    Boadicea not more bold,
And never yet the summer sun
    Lit lovelier locks of streaming gold.

A rosary of rainbow shells
    Around her beauteous neck was hung;
A mantle fair of ermine fur
    Was graceful o'er her shoulder flung.

Her eyes were of the violet's hue,
    Her lips like ripe haws on the thorn,
Her smile was like the earliest flush
    That tints the hills at early morn.

Oh, she was fair, in life's heyday,
    Riding amid her father's spears,

That maiden whose young heart's been dust
   For far above a thousand years!

The hunters now are ranked and boune,
   The priest must bless them ere they go;
They one and all on Hesus[1] call,
   And kiss the sacred mistletoe.

They then through Lochar's forest pressed,
   The crashing brushwood made them way,
And high o'erhead, through tangling boughs,
   Streamed in the radiance of the day.

Deep in the waving wild-woods rang
   The cooing of the turtle-dove,
Blent with the awful matin hymn
   Ascending from the Druid grove.

Like angel robes from heaven flung,
   The summer clouds above them roll'd;
Red as the bloom of spring's first rose,
   Their fringes tipped with living gold.

An antlered herd sprang from the copse—
   The painted hunters wild pursue;
A savage shout the welkin rent,
   And thick and fast the arrows flew.

And bounding west with reckless pace,
   Pursuing swift the antlered game,
Still fearless onward, onward rode,
   The daughter of the dauntless Graeme.

---

[1] Hesus and Bel were two of the greater Druid gods.

'Twas night. The hunters, all in sleep,
  Rested within the round stockade;
Dimly the camp-fires smouldered low
  And lurid in the midnight shade.

The warders shout a wild alarm—
  The Roman eagle streams on high:
O gods! a thousand torches flare,
  Red, wildly 'gainst the midnight sky.

They come! they come! a tortoise[1] dense—
  The arrows fall like wintry rain;
A splintered rock goes thund'ring down,
  Cleaving a crushed and bloody lane.

Yet firm and grim the Romans close,
  And, still unbroken, struggle still,
'Mid groans of death and savage yells,
  To gain the summit of the hill.

On the shield roof, with fearful clang,
  Huge stones and fiery bolts are hurled;
Yet steady up the hill they press,
  The far-famed conquerors of the world.

The hill is won; but closely pent
  Round the earth rampart and stockade,
In triple lines are warriors ranked,
  With ponderous axe and pointless blade.

---

[1] On advancing to attack an enemy, the Romans held their shields over their heads, the one shield overlapping the other, like the slates upon the roof of a house. This shield roof was called a *testudo* or *tortoise*, from its resemblance to the overlapping sections of shell on the back of that reptile. The Britons are represented as endeavouring to break this advancing roof of shields by rolling pieces of rock down the hill upon it, and by showers of stones and darts, and live coals in order to set it on fire.

Graeme.

The lines are gathered to the push—
 They reel—they form—they charge again;
They fight o'er ramparts of their dead,
 And the red life-blood pours like rain.

High rings the madd'ning neigh of steeds,
 The furious clash of sword and spear—
The rattling wheels proclaim his course,
 The wild, woad-painted charioteer.[1]

The moon gleams like a silver shield,
 High up on heaven's cloud-strewn floor,
Lighting the billowy surge of arms,
 Breaking on red Death's ghastly shore.

Godlike in might, of giant height,
 Seen by the flaring torch's flame,
Who's he far in the Roman ranks,
 Girdled with steel? 'Tis fearless Graeme!

Both hands are on his awful hilt,
 And brands and torches round him flare,
Gleaming on his uplifted arms,
 And streaming folds of auburn hair.

Terrific sweeps his red claymore,
 Alone amid a thousand foes;
Aye as he cleaves the gaps of death,
 The living billows round him close.

He's down! O gods, he's up once more!
 Crash goes the steel through helm and brain,

---

[1] The Britons punctured grotesque and frightful figures into their skins with a blue vegetable pigment called *woad*. This was in order to make them appear more terrible in battle.

Lorica[1] gives but weak defence,
   Hasta[2] and scutum[3] fly in twain !

Stern, fiercely in the torch's flare,
   Reeking and red from head to heel,
Still does that fearless heart the Graeme
   Rush on the ridge of levelled steel.

'Tis o'er—low stoops that lofty head,
   And falls for aye that sword of flame;
O Liberty ! that mangled form
   Is all now of the mighty Graeme !

And where is she, the Druid maid?
   Fainting and weary, breasting still
The ranks of steel and brazen mail
   That struggle on the Wardlaw Hill.

Behold the Druid maiden fall
   Amid the conflict's wildest roar !
Her hand still grasps the broken blade—
   With her long tresses shaded o'er.

Like summer flower by scythe cut down
   In the meadow's scented breath,
Fell the sweet rose of Niddesdale
   Under the scythe of death.

Morn sowed the world with purple light,
   And from the clouds, serene and still,

---

[1] *Lorica*, a coat of mail or brigandine.   [2] *Hasta*, a kind of spear or lance.
[3] *Scutum*, a shield or target.

Looked sorrowing down on wreck and death,
   And fatal Wardlaw's tented hill.

A Roman legion held the fort,
   Cold slept they that 'gainst mighty Rome
Dared for their rights to wield the sword
   For life, for liberty, and home.

There lay the Roman in his mail,
   And there the deer-skin mantle lay
Blood-red, where to the fearless heart
   The Roman steel had forced its way.

And grim and ghastly death was there,
   On brave men who knew how to die;
And glazèd eyes still open glared,
   As if for vengeance, to the sky.

Ah, many a Roman soldier looked
   With sorrow on the Druid maid,
Resting so calmly beautiful—
   Resting upon the shivered blade.

The mistletoe upon her brow
   Waved gently in the morning's breath,
And fresh the leaves, all dewy green,
   Lay on the pallid brow of death.

It seemed as if a balmy sleep
   Had closed the blue eyes of the fair,
The breeze upon her death-cold cheek
   Played with the ringlets of her hair.

Full many a Roman soldier found
   His comrade, lost for aye to fame,
Lining the awful lane of death,
   The sword-hewn pathway of the Graeme.

Upon a heap of dead he lay,
   His war-cry hushed for ever now,
A hundred spear-wounds in his breast,
   A wide, red gash upon his brow.

At arm's length howled in his death grasp
   The wolf, that came ere life was o'er
To tear the stalwart warrior's thews,
   Now stiff and rigid evermore.

His mangled clansmen lay behind,
   Who with him oft had breasted death,
And with him there had cleft their way,
   Till the last throb of life and breath.

Ah, well, right well Agricola knew,
   By raid, by rapine, steel, and flame,
The fearless horde that knew no creed
   But the wild slogan of the Graeme!

'Tis midnight. Doleful is the wail
   Arising from the temple stones,
In murky gloom and darkness wrapt,
   Round which the Lochar forest groans.

Through dusky night a lurid flame
   Bursts with a thousand forks on high;
Ah, Rome! the wicker cage is filled,[1]
   And there thy tortured sons must die.

---

[1] It was a custom with the Britons to force their prisoners of war into a huge basket of wattles, bearing a rough resemblance to the human form, and then to burn together the basket and those it imprisoned.

'And there they die, e'en let them die,
   In agony, far from Latium's shore;
Their agony matches not our woe,
   For oh, the gallant Graeme's no more!

'So let them die,' the Druid sang,
   'The roaring flames their funeral knell;
Their torture's grateful to the eye
   Of angry Hesus, and of Bel.

'Their smoke ascends to heaven—see
   The venging demons 'mid the gloom;
They wave their shadowy hands in wrath,
   And beckon Rome unto her doom.

'But oh, the dauntless Graeme's no more,
   The bravest warrior e'er drew breath,
Or e'er unbarred with warrior hand
   The grim and fearful door of death.

'And oh, the Graeme! the Graeme's no more,
   The stalwart Graeme our bards adored;
Then build, build high his warrior cairn,
   And lay by him his broken sword.

'O Albyn, weep—weep tears of blood;
   Sons you shall bear of might and fame,
But never, never, never more
   A warrior like the gallant Graeme!

'And oh, the stalwart Graeme's no more,
   A braver soldier ne'er drew breath,
Nor e'er unbolted with his sword
   The grim and awful gate of death!'

ERIC HAAERFAGER.

A LAY OF SAXON ENGLAND.

[A few of the specially Runic words and allusions in this poem are not here explained by footnotes. In regard to others, the reader is referred to the notes to 'The Raid of the Vikingr,' p. 20.]

BOLDLY sang the Saxon gleemen
　　This fierce lay of long ago,
While the Saxons yet were freemen,
　　Long ere Harold's overthrow.[1]

To bear off to his stormy voes [2]
　　England's Fairest of the Fair,
Was the task he did propose:
As his latest sun arose,
　　This was bold Haaerfager's prayer:—

'O Odin, red Odin, thou god of the battle,
　　Come listen to me 'mong the ghosts of Valhalla!
'Mong the mountains of dead my ancestors bled,
　　'Mid the groan and the yell and the shout of Braavalla![3]

'And fierce Sigard's hair—ay, his long hoary hair—
　　Fell, to wave o'er the wilds of the Nordland no more;
And hosts closed their eyes on the earth and the skies,
　　'Fore my forefather, bold Harold Ganger of yore!

'His hand all imbrued from the war with the Swede,
　　He raised his right arm and triumphantly swore:
" No well-gallied fiord shall e'er see my sword,
　　It will never more flash on the Anglian shore!

---

[1] The overthrow of the Saxons under Harold II. at Hastings, 1066.
[2] *Voes*, creeks or inlets of the sea.
[3] Battle of Braavalla, A.D. 740, where Harold Goldtooth, the Dane, defeated Sigard Ring, king of Sweden. Sigard, old and blind, fell in the engagement, and Harold ruled in Scandinavia.

' " I'll die in the noon of my glory to-day;
    I'll die like a Dane on this field of Braavalla;
To-night my red fingers shall redden the skull
    That's lifted on high to the toast in Valhalla!

' " My sun's at its height, shall I wait the decline?"
    And he fell on his sword, calling Odin and Thor:
His spirit forth rushed as his bosom's blood gushed,
    And his great gallant heart was still evermore!

'And, O Odin, oft his descendant, Haaerfager,
    Has met the seaxe of the Saxon afar;
His yellow hair wet with the red battle sweat,
    In the autumn of Death—in the harvest of War!

'Then, oh, if the lives he has laid at your shrine,
    If the dints on the casque that encircles his brow
Have e'er you delighted, let his suit be not slighted,
    But grant the petition he brings to you now!

'Rowena is fair as the flash of the morn,
    When Heimdal[1] looks down from the rim of the day,
'Mong the dark, groaning pines where the Norsemen are born,
    And the ocean of mist, slowly melting away.

' Her brow is as white as the wastes of the snow
    On the peaks of the Kolen, tremendous and high,
When the breath of midnight lifts the curtain of white,
    And mingles its folds with the stars of the sky.

---

[1] Heimdal, the god with the golden teeth. He was stationed at one end of the bridge of Bifrost, which reached from earth to heaven. There he defended the bridge against the giants. He was the gonfalonier or standard-bearer of the gods. His hearing was such that he heard the grass growing in the fields, and he saw for a hundred leagues either by night or day. The sound of his trumpet might be heard through the universe.

'Great Odin, then help, and the maid shall be mine,
   ThoughI wade to her bower to the sword-belt in gore;
Down the arch of Bifrost,[1] come, Odin the Mighty,
   As I gird on my sword on the Anglian shore.'

At eve before Udolf's strong ramparts they stood,
   And the warder replied to a blast at the gate:
'Let Count Beowulf know that one waits him below,
   A peer to the bravest and best in your state!'

Then high from the rampart Count Beowulf cried:
   'Who art thou, O warrior, that waits me below?
A proud Scottish thane? Art thou Norseman or Dane?—
   Sir knight, answer quickly, if friend or if foe?'

'Beowulf, I have come from a far foreign land;
   Red gold, gallant hearts, and strong castles are mine:
I've crossed land and water for the fair daughter,
   Bretwalda, for that young Rowena of thine.

'I'll love her as never a maiden was loved—
   By our god, Beowulf, what makes you thus start?
I'll defend her, her lord, with a warrior's sword,
   And love with the might of a warrior's heart!'

'Be yours, courteous stranger? This never can be;
   She's espoused to her kinsman, this daughter of mine:
By all that is dear, by Hengist's red spear,
   The blue-eyed Rowena can never be thine!'

'Bethink you, Bretwalda; disguised as a bard,
   At Yule in last year I harped in your hall,
And my heart thrilled on fire as my hand struck the lyre,
   And I gazed on the maid from a niche in the wall.

'Udolf, ever since, and wherever I've fought,
   She's haunted me ever, wherever I've strayed,

[1] See preceding note.

Like the morning sunbeam—like a joy in a dream,
  The beautiful form of the young Saxon maid.

And I thought, Beowulf, that a high heart like thine
  Its countenance, favour, and gift ever gave
To the best arm and sword, and deemed the best lord
  Was he clasped his love to the breast of the brave.'

'You were right, noble stranger,' young Cerda replied
  ('Twas he was espoused to Rowena the Fair);
'And he may bear the prize, by Rowena's bright eyes,
  Who's braver than Cerda to do and to dare!

'There you have your broadsword, and here I have mine,
  Come, we'll throw the dice for a bride or a grave;
And let him be lord who owns the best sword,
  And let his love rest on the breast of the brave.'

'By the beauty of Balder, the hammer of Thor,[1]
  I'll meet you anon, or lay me with Vala,[2]
Ay, and close, double-barred, spite of all I have warred,
  Against me for ever the gate of Valhalla.

---

[1] The hammer of Thor was kept always red-hot, and was of such a weight that it required ten men to carry it on a hurdle. It was once stolen by the giants while Thor was asleep, and buried eight miles deep in Giantland. The gods, anxious for the recovery of the hammer, resorted to the following artifice. They negotiated concerning a marriage of Freya, their goddess of love, with the chief of the giants. It was stipulated that the hammer should be produced at the marriage. Thor dressed himself like and personated Freya; but the giants expressed their astonishment at the voracious appetite of the bride, when she did more than justice to the viands by eating eight salmon and an entire ox. According to contract, the hammer was produced, when the bride (Thor) seized it with a savage shout of triumph, and dealt with it an indiscriminate carnage among the deluded giants.

[2] Vala, the writer of the *Voluspa*, the most ancient of the sacred writings of the Scandinavians. The body of Vala lay near the eastern gate of Niflheim:
  'Hard by the eastern gate of hell,
    In ancient times great Vala fell.'—HERBERT'S *Helga*.

'And know, haughty Saxon, base keeper of swine,[1]
　My falchion is worthy to find you a grave ;
Let your cheek blanch with fear—hear, tremble to hear—
　I'm ERIC HAAERFAGER—HAAERFAGER THE BRAVE !'

'Haaerfager the Brave ! Red demon-berserker ![2]
　By the tomb where King Jesus in victory lay,
Meet this keeper of swine ; for on your eyes or mine
　This even the sunlight is setting for aye !'

'Son of the land of the jarl and the kraken,[3]
　Red glory is dearer than being and breath ;
Let the Scaldic harp ring of my falchion's swing
　To the spell-word of Eric, "Rowena or Death !"'

Terrific the blows on the habergeon fall,
　The plumes are shorn off and the war-chargers bound ;
But Cerda's steed reels, his foe on him wheels,
　The horse of the Saxon is borne to the ground.

But Cerda arises and Eric dismounts ;
　They struggle, they grapple in rage and despair ;
Stern, wild they strike on—Eric's helmet is gone,
　And ruddy drops drip from his long yellow hair.

And the blood and the foam through the joints of their mail
　Render slippery the turf and the hilt of the glave ;
God ! How long shall it last, ere the die may be cast—
　And whose is Rowena? and whose is the grave?

The even hangs dim on the grapple of Death,
　On the fire-sparks that fly from the blade and the mail ;

[1] The keeping of swine was one of the principal national industries of the Saxons.
[2] The berserkers fought without armour in a state of semi-nudity, and with the most reckless bravery.
[3] Kraken, a huge imaginary sea monster seen off the shores of Scandinavia.

Like a ghost from a shroud, the moon through a cloud
    Shines weird on the deep crimsoned grass of the vale.

Ho! shout for young Cerda, for Cerda the Saxon,
    And honour, old England, his heart and his hand,
The darling of freemen, the theme of the gleemen,
    The glory of Deira,[1] the pride of the land!

Hurrah! it is over, the Norseman is down—
    His spirit now howls on the borean shore;
Ho! carry the tidings to hamlet and town,
    That the hard-striking Eric will strike nevermore!

Count Beowulf's vassals have taken his Norse,
    And stung them with snakes in the dank dungeon gloom,[2]
Then, at dead of the night, by the torches' red light,
    Laid their black swollen corses at rest in the tomb.

Three days and three nights the head of Haaerfager
    In triumph, impaled on the point of his sword,
The young Cerda bore till he reached the wild shore
    Where the Norsemen lay waiting for Eric their lord.

'Twas night: he beheld o'er a beetling cliff
    The horde of berserkers, their fires all aglow;
He hurled down the head, all mangled and red,
    Down to the camp of the corsairs below.

Down hurled the head o'er the brow of the cliff,
    It crashed through the night-shade and thyme as it fell,
And the tangled briers tear the long matted hair:
    Hark! shrieks rise as if from the torment of hell.

---

[1] Deira, one of the Saxon kingdoms into which England was divided.

[2] This instance of revolting cruelty to a vanquished enemy is not without precedent, and only refers to a species of torture literally resorted to in these barbarous times. Regnar Lodbrok, son of Sigard Ring, being seized and imprisoned by Ella, king of Sussex, shouted his war-cry and chanted martial sagas while snakes were stinging him to death in the dungeon.

'Haaerfager's proud head from the stars of the heaven!
  Great Thor, it is Eric—broad brow and wild eye!
We'll buy not a wind[1]—leave this curst shore behind—
  We cannot the arm of the demons defy!'

Precipitate fled to their galleys the Norse,
  A league and a half off, a-riding the wave,
Till corses threescore, 'mid the wreck on the shore,
  Next morn lay the heroes of Eric the Brave!

Ho! shout for young Cerda, for Cerda the Saxon,
  And honour, old England, his heart and his hand—
The darling of freemen, the theme of the gleemen,
  The glory of Deira, the pride of the land!

RAID OF THE VIKINGR.

[ODIN or WODEN was the god of war—the chief god among the Scandinavians. We still have his name in *Wednesday* (= *Woden's day*), and in *Wednesburgh* (= *Woden's burgh* or *town*). The Norsemen despised the Christians, who, they said, worshipped a *white Christ*, full of pity and compassion and long-suffering, while they exulted in their homage to Odin, who delighted in blood and rapine and slaughter.—The *Vikingr* were so called from *vik*, a creek. They lay in these creeks in their long war-boats, hence their name. (The word has no relation to *king*.) *Vikingr* is the plural, the oldest form of which plural was in *ru*. We still find this form in *heronry*, *falconry*, *eyry*, and other words.]

THE Raven, the Raven is dark on the gale
That wrathfully roars through the cordage and sail;
At the black dragon-prow[2] the ocean is dashing,
On the storm-battered deck shields and cymbals are clashing;

---

[1] The buying and selling of winds to effect prosperous voyages was a regular commercial transaction among the old 'sea-kings,' who seldom ventured upon any maritime enterprise of importance without purchasing a prosperous wind. The chief vendors were old women accredited with supernatural influence, and occupying something like the position occupied by *witches* in mediæval Christendom.

[2] The Norse galleys were built in the form of a dragon, the head projecting at the prow, and the tail raised aloft at the stern.

And 'Hurrah and hurrah!' shout the sons of the main,
And swells the broad chest of the steel-shirted Dane;
And the roar of the chant drowns the roar of the sea—
'War-hammer, war-axe, and red Odin for me!'

Their axes are swinging, their brass shields are ringing;
They quaff horns of mead, and they stretch to the oar,
While their sagas[1] keep time in terrible chime
To the whirls of the ocean that boil evermore;
And Hilda the dear one, and Brenda the fair,
Named in sagas of love or of terrible glee,
Mix again and again with the awful refrain,
'The ocean, my galley, and Odin for me!'

A heap of red cinders, bespattered with blood,
Marks where the thane's castle rose sternly at morn;
And dashed is the rood from the height where it stood,
On the loftiest tower of the Abbey of Thorn.[2]
On Gurth's ruined grange the barn is on fire,
The barley's ablaze on the upland and lea;
Louder, louder the song peals wrathful and strong,—
'No white Christ, but Odin, red Odin for me!'

And the Raven and Horse[3] are met in the dell,
With spiked club and axe-swing, with groan and with yell.
The wolf and the crow—they wait for the dead,
Where the flowers of the mead bloom in one horrid red;

---

[1] *Sagas*, the songs or ballads of the Scandinavians, a people passionately fond of warlike minstrelsy.

[2] Where Westminster Abbey stands was formerly a small island, formed by a curve of the Thames, known as the Isle of Thorn. Before it was occupied by a Christian church, it was the site of a Roman temple to Apollo.

[3] The *raven* was the insignia on the standard of the Norseman, the *white horse* on that of the Saxon.

And the lays of the scalds[1] peal awful and high,
And the valkyry[2] ring of the Norse battle-cry,
'Niflheim,[3] frigid hell for the Dane that will flee!—
No Christ but the Nordland's red Odin for me!'

Ah! redder now flushes the wild rose's bud,
And the eye of the daisy is blinded in blood.
Now England, prepare for raid, rapine, and lust,
For your gallant White Horse lies low in the dust!
Victorious the jarl sings of Balder[4] and Thor,[5]
And the souls of the brave that return never more:
'Ho, yell of the battle and roar of the sea,—
War-hammer, war-axe, and red Odin for me!'

THE MINSTREL KING.

IT was inside the savage camp
   Of jarls of field and flood,
Whose ruthless blades had freely drank,
   And deep, of Saxon blood:

---

[1] The *Scalds* were the poets or bards of the Norsemen.

[2] The *Valkyries* were the goddesses of slaughter, who, before an engagement, selected those who should be slain. They conducted the souls of the fallen to Valhalla, and were the cup-bearers of the gods.

[3] *Niflheim*, the Scandinavian hell, not of fiery torment, but consisting of nine concentric circles of ice, the cold increasing and intensifying in the direction of the innermost circle.

[4] *Balder*, a son of Odin. On the columns of his palace were engraven rhymes supposed to have power to reanimate the dead. He was shot dead by an arrow of mistletoe, discharged by his blind brother Hoder.

[5] *Thor* was the eldest and bravest of the sons of Odin and Freya. Wonderful feats are attributed to him, of which the following may serve as a specimen:—The giants having challenged Thor to drink out of their great horn, he felt piqued at being able to drain it only to the depth of a few feet. The giants, however, expressed their amazement at his prowess, for they confessed to having taken the bottom out of the horn, and to having submerged the bottomless end in the sea. So Thor had drunk the entire ocean shallower by several feet!

The Minstrel King.

King Guthrum sat upon his throne,
    As neared the day's decline,
And ' Let us quaff,' the monarch cried,
    'The victor's blood-red wine;
We are masters of the island,
    From east to western shore,
And the Pale Horse [1] of the Saxon
    Is down for evermore!

'The plains have now been soaked and wet
    With slaughter's crimson rain,
And over ev'ry fortress waves
    The Raven [2] of the Dane:
Come, fill the goblet brimming high—
    We'll drink from skulls ere long; [3]
But while we drain the flowing bowl,
    Come, soul of martial song;
Where is the Minstrel? Bring him forth,
    To hear him I am fain;
And bid him sing, in martial strain,
    The glory of the Dane!

' And bid him sing of Hilda's charms,
    Of Dagmar's locks of gold,
Of galleys on the dashing sea,
    Of glorious deeds of old;
Of valkyries [4] that tell the dead
    Upon the battle morn,

---

[1] The *Pale Horse* was the insignia upon the Saxon standard.

[2] The *Raven* was the insignia upon the Danish standard.

[3] One of the delights of the Scandinavian heaven was for the blessed to drink blood out of the skulls of those whom they had slain in battle upon earth.

[4] *Valkyries*, the goddesses of slaughter, who before the armies engaged in battle marked out those who were doomed to fall. *Vide* note on previous page.

And of the flaming Christian church
    Upon the Isle of Thorn;[1]
How the faith of peaceful Jesus
    Is uprooted evermore,
And the flag of mighty Odin
    Now waves from shore to shore.'

In Alfred strode,—the Saxon king,—
    Arrayed in minstrel guise,
But round the hostile camp there ranged
    His dark and piercing eyes;
He ev'ry point of weakness scanned,
    Where Saxon force might gain,
By main and might, in desperate fight,
    A victory o'er the Dane;
But on he sang of heroes dead,
    And widows left forlorn,—
And well the Minstrel King foresaw
    A wild and awful morn.

His lay portrayed the Danish axe
    In horrid circle wheel,
The clanking, clashing miles on miles
    Of rasping, dripping steel;
The Raven up, the White Horse down,
    The grass all slippery red,
And helm and cuish, blade and spur,
    Commingled with the dead;
And laurels and Valhalla for
    The never-dying brave,
Who passed to Thor and Odin
    Through the portal of the grave!

The stars before the morning rise
    Were gleaming sharp and clear,

[1] Westminster Abbey originally stood on the Isle of Thorn.

The Danish camp-lights dimly fell
    On shield, and axe, and spear:
The Minstrel was a warrior now,
    And thousands fenced him round,
Right cautious in the dark they crept
    Along the battle ground;
Then pealed a shout of thunder power--
    The land is free again!
And the Pale Horse has triumphed o'er
    The Raven of the Dane!

EDITH.

[Ancient chronicles record that the body of King Harold, as it lay on the field of Hastings, was so defaced with wounds that it could not be identified, till at length it was recognised by Edith (of the Swan Neck), a young lady of the king's household.]

BRETWALDA, noble Harold! death's dark red roses blow
O'er the winter plain of Senlac—the mighty lying low.
Bretwalda, Edith seeks you—Edith you loved of yore,
The gold spangles of her slippers incarnadine with gore!

Alas, O race of Hengist! and alas! its evil star,
In ruin set, shall blaze no more over the field of war!
O Harold! wild and glorious has thy life's course been driven
From hence to meet Hardraga on the golden floor of heaven!

For but the brave may meet thee, wherever thou art now:
No earthly crown was grand enough for thy broad kingly brow;
And no steel blade was true enough to grace thy warrior thigh;
No paladin was worthy for thee to dare and die.

And but the fair may meet thee, wherever thou may'st be:
Alas! earth's best and fairest were all unworthy thee;
And ne'er shall England's maidens find in all the conquering race
The beauty even death has left upon thy manly face!

I kiss thee, son of Godwin; 'tis the last for evermore,—
Forget not Saxon Edith upon the eternal shore;
When all the harps of God are struck in heaven to welcome thee,
My Harold—Saxon Harold—oh, then remember me!

Think on the hush of summer eve, on the earth so far away,
When gleamed through England's leafy oaks the sheen of dying day
On Harold and on Edith, in young life's budding glow,
Ere darkened merry England this night of death and woe!

Lo, the midnight clouds are scattered by wild October's breath,
And the Star of Love looks down on the stricken field of death,
As though the might of Meekness would the sword of Hate defy,—
A glory burning on the cope of the everlasting sky.

Ah! the hate of Norman William can never reach you there;
But in the holy fields of heaven may Saxon Edith's prayer,
With memories of dear England, the land that gave you birth,
Sweet whispers of the sunshine and the green leaves of the earth.

There are moanings from the slaughter-heaps and voices in the air—
A death-cold hand is lying 'mong the tangles of my hair.
Young Harold! England's hero-king! thine is the soldier's grave,
And the immortal name that marks the manhood of the brave!

HEREWARD.

[Hereward was the last Englishman ('Saxon') of note who made any stand against the power of William the Conqueror after the battle of Hastings. He was the son of Leofric, Lord of Brun, in East Anglia. While yet a mere boy, he gave evidence of determined bravery and great physical strength; but his will was uncurbed, and his love of chivalric adventure far exceeded the bounds of discretion, and occasionally bade defiance to the laws of the realm. By the time he grew up to manhood, his restless spirit and terrible arm, highly celebrated even in an age of physical prowess and daring, had involved his father in such difficulties and entanglements that he was constrained to request Edward the Confessor to pronounce a sentence of outlawry against his ungovernable son, Hereward. Thus exiled, after several adventures in several lands, Hereward passed over into Flanders, and plunged into the war raging in that country.

After the Conquest he returned to England. He found his father dead, and the castle of Brun occupied by a Norman knight, named Taillebois.[1] Collecting a few of his old retainers who had escaped slaughter, this desperate son of the sword attempted to wrest Brun Castle by storm from the hated Norman. He was repulsed, and the Norman troops assembled in such force round the point of attack that the brave Englishman felt compelled to retreat from before the towers of his ancestors. Like Alfred, he sought a retreat in the fens of Ely, where, in the middle of a quaking and all but impassable bog, he established what was called the 'Camp of Refuge,' a wooden structure to which a number of hunted and outlawed Englishmen followed him. From the Camp of Refuge as a centre, Hereward kept up an irregular but harassing warfare upon the neighbouring districts. So unprecedented and reckless was the nature of his incursions, that he became an object of apprehension even to the stern and resolute Conqueror himself, who well knew that the English people were vanquished but not subdued, and that it only required the fitting opportunity and the presence of a leader like Hereward to raise insurrections which might imperil even his crown. Accordingly, William in person visited the Ely fen. His practised eye at once took in the whole situation. He ordered that a solid causeway, two miles in length, should be built across the swamps right into the Camp of Refuge. This was set about, but it proved a task of no ordinary difficulty. Hereward and his followers fell upon the workmen and the soldiers who supported them, till relay after relay had to be sent to take the place of the slaughtered, and carry forward the fatal causeway. Soldiers and workmen alike became impressed with the idea that, from the resistless strength of his arm, Hereward was more than a mere mortal, and had entered into alliance with Satan, to whom, and not to Hereward himself, the feats of strength and bravery were attributed. Accordingly, to counteract and to foil this power of the Evil One, a wooden tower, containing a witch, was pushed forward to the extremity of the causeway. The soldiers deemed themselves safe under her protection, and the poor old woman brandished her withered arms and shrieked her incantations. Laughing her to scorn, Hereward again fell,

---

[1] This word now appears in English as *Talboys*. It was the Norman-French for *wood-cutter* (from *tailler*, to cut). So also *taillefer*, a sword-smith, which has become our word *Telfer*.

sword in hand, upon the Normans; and having set fire to the harvest of tall and dry withered reeds, the wretched woman was burnt to death. Many others, their clothes having caught fire, perished as they ran about madly in the blinding smoke and quaking fen.

At length, however, as the old chroniclers relate, the monks of Ely led the Normans by stealth into the Camp of Refuge by a way known only to Hereward and his friends. The heroic Englishman, thus betrayed, offered, as was his wont, a gallant resistance; but at length, perceiving further opposition to be useless, he cut his way through the ranks of his enemies and effected his escape. What was his ultimate fate is doubtful; but it is on record that his death was in keeping with his life,—that, taken by surprise and at disadvantage by twenty Norman knights, unsupported and alone, he yet fought with such strength and courage that sixteen of the twenty perished beneath his arm. Then, covered with wounds and faint with loss of blood, he struggled with the remaining four till at length their weapons were buried in his unconquerable heart.]

ENGLAND, my bleeding country,
    Give me a thousand men—
As whilom followed Alfred
    Into this dismal fen:
Give back a thousand of the brave
    Who fell on Senlac Hill,
And once again old England
    Will be *our* England still.

In vain—in vain!—the voiceless grave
    Responds not to my call;
No hero bursts the dusty tomb
    To man the leaguered wall,—
To struggle in the front with me
    Once more for England's crown,
And aid to dash, with reddened axe,
    The Norman standard down!

A foreign tongue is spoken now
    Within our ancient hall,
Far other feasts adorn the board,
    And other shields the wall:

Ancestral Brun! thy trees were green,
    And fair thy rippling streams;
Scene of my sainted mother's love,
    My boyhood's daring dreams.

But my veins surged at fever heat,
    My heart beat proud and high;
I yearned, I burned to glorious live,
    Or yet more glorious die:
No rattle pleased me when a babe,
    'Twas the trumpet's sternest call;
E'en then the dearest toy I knew
    Was the war-axe on the wall.

Anon I heard the gleeman's lay
    Of deeds on land and sea,
Till earth, with all its mighty girt,
    Became too small for me:
Oh, to burst from my quiet home
    To the broad noon-day of fame,
Till the gleeman's song and the gleeman's **lyre**
    Should ring with Hereward's name!

'Old England, thou hast not,' I said,
    'Of toil and strife enow;
I'll seek in mightier fields to win
    A laurel for my brow.'
Enough! in sooth I had to go,
    By an edict from the throne—
Of all that appertained to me,
    I took my sword alone.

'Tis not for me to tell my deeds,
    Or how my blood was poured;
And how the kings of Europe bade
    For Hereward and his sword:

How, covered with renown in arms,
   I sought my native shore,
To find I had no country—
   I had a home no more.

O England, had I stood by thee
   In thy dire hour of ill,
And led on my father's vassals
   To Senlac's awful hill,
And dashed sheer at the Norman front
   With a thousand Lincoln men,
Not all the might of Normandy
   Had routed Harold then!

The war I wage is hopeless,
   And that full well I know;
It but remains to sell my life
   Full dearly to the foe:
And ne'er shall, Hereward living,
   The Pale Horse flag be furl'd—
One sword and one heroic heart
   Against a banded world!

THE AMPULLA.

A LEGEND OF THOMAS À BECKET.

[Among the regalia preserved in the Tower, there is the *ampulla*, or golden eagle, for the consecrated oil with which the king is anointed at his coronation. A singular tradition regarding the ampulla states that it was brought by the Virgin to Thomas à Becket, while he was praying in a church at Sens during his banishment. The Virgin, at the same time, gave the saint a small phial, and assured him that the kings anointed from it would be happy and prosperous.]

IN tears before the altar rail
   The exiled Becket lay,
While dimly on his cord and cowl
   Streamed in the light of day—

Streamed faintly through the painted glass,
   In soft and solemn flow,
And slumbered on the broad, dark stones
   That hid the dead below,—
The dead that in the aisle of Sens
   Were buried long ago.

And drear and deep were Becket's moans,
   As on those flags he lay;
And, high among the hills of heaven,
   The angels heard him pray;
His voice echoed sepulchral
   Beneath the hollow stone—
The prayer for England's altar,
   The sigh for England's throne.

The marble-cold Madonna
   Looked on à Becket's woe
From behind her snowy drapery,
   In that church of long ago;
And the breath of the Almighty struck
   That marble, cold and white,
And glared red through the church of Sens
   A more than earthly light;
And all the dead below the stones
   Waked in their dreamless night.

Down from the niche the Virgin stepped,
   As the ancient legends say,
And moved, in sculptured majesty,
   To the stone where Becket lay,
And past the altar pix and cross
   Held her unearthly way:
The snow-white stone that made her lips
   Assumed the rose's hue,

The marble eyes grew clear and calm
    As morning's pearly dew;
Her bosom heaved, her garment flowed,
    She breathed the summer air;
The evening threw a golden flash
    Upon her streaming hair.

'All hail!' the marble Virgin said,
    'Rise from thy bended knee,—
Thou'rt entered in the roll of heaven,
    To die for God and me:
I see thee, on the altar steps,
    Fall back to rise no more,
I see that lofty fane in Kent [1]
    Red with thy saintly gore,
And martyr-glory like to thine
    Was never known before.
The harp-strings in the halls of God
    Shall lose their primal tone,
The hymnal round the Throne shall change,
    As eternity rolls on:
When warriors of the sword of steel
    Are dead and vulgar clay,
And history points but dimly
    To their weird and stormy day,
Thou, soldier of a mightier sword,
    Shall flash far through the gloom,—
In every brain thy memory,
    In every heart thy tomb.

'Bleeding, 'mong Calvary's olive trees,
    In agony died my Son,
That, blot among a million worlds,
    This earth should back be won—

---

[1] Canterbury Cathedral, where à Becket was murdered, 1170.

The Ampulla.

Won back to be a world of bliss,
   Instead of bane and doom—
He, dying, took the sting from Death,
   The terror from the tomb:
And o'er all hills Mount Calvary
   Stands glorious, bright, divine,
There hangs a halo not of earth
   O'er her olive and her vine
That halo, somewhat dimmer,
   Shall light the altar stone,
Where, loyal friend to England's Church,
   Hence foe to England's throne,
Thy blood, thy heart's blood, Becket
   (Thy floors by murderers trod),
Shall rush out under ruffian blades
   In martyrdom to God!

'Take thou this sacred eagle,
   Take it to thy island home;
And the Beauty of old Greece,
   And the Might of ancient Rome,
Shall dwindle into nothingness
   'Fore the great, the grand, the free,
The focus-light of all the world—
   The England that's to be!
Lo, the future on my soul
   A prophetic vision flings—
A PEOPLE greater than their isle,
   And grander than their kings—
Harnessing fire, wielding the winds,
   And the lightnings of the sky,—
The only spear in all the land,
   The spear upon the rye!

'Take, holy man, this eagle,
   This pledge of gold, from me,

And this phial, filled in heaven
   From the dew upon the tree
That, blooming in eternity,
   Throws odour, shade, and balm
Upon the choir that sing the song
   Of Moses and the Lamb!'

Dumb and bewildered Becket rose,
   And crossed to England's shore;
With him the golden eagle
   And phial-gift he bore,
And hastened to the fane in Kent
   That soon, with martyr gore,
Reeked under stabs of murderous swords,
   As the Virgin had foretold,
When the martyr prayed at holy Sens
   In the saintly days of old.

And, even to this very day,
   From nations far and wide,
Men come and look with pious awe
   On the spot where Becket died;
And to this day the eagle,
   And the phial filled with dew,
Are seen in London's ancient Tower,
   To prove the legend true—
The consecrated phial,
   And the eagle all of gold—
Dim relics of the mysteries
   Of the saintly days of old.

RICHARD LION-HEART.

A LAY OF THE CRUSADES.

[At Ascalon, Richard I. was seized with fever. But even severe illness could not abate the warlike ardour of his temperament; and when he could no longer stand upon his feet, he ordered that he should be carried in front of the walls on a litter, that he might superintend operations, and incite the Christians to a vigorous prosecution of the siege.]

'Ha! ha! my veins are raging hot,
    My hectic senses reel!
Pshaw, fever! Bring my harness, squire,
    My morion of steel.
I cannot live supine like this,
    And die like coward slave
Ho, reeling front of battle be
    The death-bed of the brave!

'No, no, my Berengaria!
    Take that bandage from my head,
And bring me, gentle wife of mine,
    The iron helm instead:
And put thy snow-white favour
    In my plume, so dark and high;
Steel harness be my winding-sheet,
    A soldier let me die!

'Know, in this sainted Palestine
    The Saviour died for me;
And my good sword and strong right arm
    Shall strike for Him and thee;
And ne'er shall heathen sandals tread,
    And heathen banners wave,
O'er the garden of His agony,
    The glory of His grave!

No! o'er the Moslem turban,
    And the flashing scimitar,
We'll pour the hosts of England
    In the thunder-crash of war.
On, warriors of the high crusade,
    Bended bow and swinging sword,—

And wave o'er Pagan Ascalon
   The banner of the Lord!

'Gird on my heavy armour,
   Bring my war-horse from the stall;
Sound the trumpet, shout Jehovah!
   Forward, onward to the wall!
Come, gentle Berengaria,—
   Through the vizor bars a kiss;
And I'll leave to weak old women
   A dying bed like this.

'Let Leopold of Austria
   Die thus, when die he may;
Let craven Philip breathe his last
   Far from the battle fray;
The couch of Richard Lion-heart
   Must be the crimson sod,
Where, 'neath the bannered cross, he fought
   For glory and for God.

'See, holy Carmel's dark with shame,
   Red blushes Jordan's tide,
That Saladin should hold a day
   The land where Jesus died;
Ho! where the dead lie thickest
   Upon earth's groaning breast,
At eve search for King Richard,
   And lay him to his rest!

'And not in dear old England
   Lay you your leader dead,
But deep within this holy land
   Lay you his helmèd head;
Not English oak, but Syrian palm,
   Shall guard his soldier's grave

In the sainted land he lived to love—
   The land he died to save!

'O Salem, for thy Holy Tomb,
   O England, for thy throne,
King Death shall find King Richard
   With his armour girded on;
He'll greet thee, King of Terrors,
   O'er Jordan's mortal flood,
With a forehead wreathed in laurel,
   And a hand imbrued in blood!

'Come, laggard knights, I charge you,
   Haste, ere the sun go down,
And bear me on your shoulders
   To the ramparts of the town!—
Plunge him amid the battle shock,
   The grapple, yell, and groan,
That Death may find King Richard
   With his armour girded on!'

THE RINGLET OF LENORE.

A LEGEND OF THE CRUSADES.

'Ye starke and hawtane Macuswald,
   Thane o' Stra-Nid sae greane,
Had graithed him wi' ye holy Crosse,
   To fare wi' Ynglande's Kynge.'
               Ancient Metrical Romance.

THE tekbir yelled by Kedron's stream,
   And the Paynim scimitar
Flashed thirsting 'neath the midnight stars
   For the crimson rain of war.

The turbans gleamed like fields of snow
   On Gehenna's funeral sod,
And the Crescent waved in the pale moonbeam
   For Mahomet and God.

Dark in the smile of the silver moon,
   From their native land afar,
Lay Europe's crested chivalry—
   The ranks of the Holy War.

Dark o'er them flapped the crimson Cross,
   O'er Judah waving wide—
The Cross brought back to the dear land
   Where the Redeemer died.

'Twas the soldier's awful slumber
   On the margin of his grave;
'Twas the night—but what *the morrow*
   To the legions of the brave?

Ah, hence to gain renown on earth
   And glory in the sky,
Freely my own green Nithsdale sent
   Her sons to bleed and die.

With clanking arms and waving plume,
   Caerlaverock's portals pour
Her blooming youth, her manhood's pride,
To leave the Nith's for Jordan's side,
To come back o'er the ocean wide,
   And—to come back no more!

To have for Scotland's bonnie broom,
   The tangled Syrian vine—
To change for Solway's sea-pinks sweet,
   The myrrh of Palestine.

The Ringlet of Lenore.

And to exchange the auld kirkyaird
   And the wild rose's bloom
For a cold grave so far away,
   The trench, the soldier's tomb.

Young Eustace from the green Stra-Nid,
   In the torch-illumined air,
Pressed fondly to his boyish lips
   A tress of yellow hair.

The youth was of the Maxwell's blood,—
   An arm in fight more strong
Might not be in the serried ranks
   Of great Cœur-de-Lion.

His age was barely twenty-two,
   Yet, in the billowy fight,
Before his glave full oft the brave
   Had bade the world good-night.

And now, 'mid acton, sword, and lance,
   On Judah's holy shore,
The youth pressed in his steel-gloved hand
   The ringlet of Lenore.

'Ah, bards of future years shall sing,
   How, in the wars of yore,
Reeking and red, o'er hills of dead,
   The Cross of God I bore,
Worthy of my ancestral line,
   And worthy of Lenore!

'The laurel green upon my brow,
   I'll dally in her bowers,
And hang this good crusader's sword
   Up in my father's towers.

'My ladye's locks of streaming gold
   Shall o'er my bosom play,
Her smile repay me for the toils
   Of many a fearful day.

'Her lute shall dim the memories
   Of warfare's stern alarms;
Her gentle words, the splintering lance;
   Her song, the clash of arms.'

'Twas ruddy morn, a bloody morn,
   And mightily charged with doom—
A morning not of joy and life,
   But agony and the tomb!

Wildly the Cross and the Crescent streamed
   O'er battle's billowy wave,
And steel blades rasped in Death's mad dance—
   The grim reel of the grave!

And banners sank and banners rose,
   And, over hills of slain,
The Paynim floundered, wavered, fled,
   And wheeling, charged again!

The turbaned hosts of Saladin
   Toiled till the close of day,
And the crusader's clotted axe
   Hewed slaughter's awful way!
And still, where raged the fiercest fight,
   'Mid battle's hoarsest roar,
Was seen the shearing sword that struck
   For God and for Lenore!

They toiled and died, foot set to foot
   On the slippery grass and red,
And, blood-wet shod, the living scaled
   The ramparts of the dead!

   .   .   .   .

The moon shone on the wreck of death
   Strewn on the mournful shore;
The fated paladin beheld
   That silver moon no more:
Cold he lay on the stricken field
   With the Cross of God he bore,
And, gleaming on his gallant breast,
   The ringlet of Lenore!

THE RED-CROSS KNIGHT.

A LAY OF THE CRUSADES.

'O LADYE JANE, give a golden tress
   Ere thy Gilbert goes afar,
Along with thy father Hildebrand,
   To fight in the Holy War!'

The air had the rosy breath of June,
   The shades of the evening fell;
The young girl clasped her Gilbert's neck,
   And wept as she sighed 'Farewell!'

For a long, long year her orisons
   She daily said for him,
And devoutly sang for his soul and sword
   In the holy convent hymn.

As she dreamed in sleep in her turret high,
   All under the midnight stars,

Her Gilbert's shade appeared by her bed,
    Afar from the Holy Wars.

His beaver dark was claspèd down,
    But Gilbert's voice she knew,
And drearily a hearse-like plume
    Above his morion flew.

He laid his cold hand on her breast,—
    His hand all gloved in mail:
'Oh, art thou sleeping, Ladye Jane?—
    Wild sweeps the midnight gale!

'Behold thy Red-Cross knight once more!
    O ladye, dost thou hear?
Oh, dark is the path through the world of souls,—
    The path that brought me here!

'Dread was the sweep of the scimitar
    On Zion's sacred crown;
The warm blood gushed, the chargers rushed,
    And the Red-Cross knights went down.

'And Gilbert toiled in the battle crash,
    His grasp on the reddened glave,
And wildly mowed through the Paynim ranks
    The harvest of the grave.

'Pressing through Acre's awful breach,
    My mailed foot slipt in gore,
And through my brain, from brow to chin,
    A Pagan weapon shore.

'And o'er my corse, with slippery feet,
    Men rushed with might and main,
Till, trampled shapeless, I was left
    With Death—and Ladye Jane.

'Then thundered down the city wall,
   Beneath the brazen ram;
The rampart fell across my chest,—
   Yet, ladye, here I am!

'And then the fire of very hell
   Raged o'er the ruin drear,
And I was burnt to scorching dust,—
   Yet, ladye, I am here!

'Now, by the vow ye plighted me
   Down by the sunlit wave,
Come, my betrothed, my bride to be,
   Down in the sunless grave.

'Oh, few, few stars peep through the clouds
   That hurry o'er the sky;
But such beseems a gentle one
   Who wanders forth to die.

'The wind roars through the lonely woods,
   The billows lash the shore,
The tower to its foundation shakes
   As it ne'er shook before,

'And such a wild and gloomy night,
   Oh, never met your eye;
But such beseems a gentle one
   Who wanders forth to die!

 'Tis dreary, dreary on the shore,
   No moonbeams on the hill;
The fire-forms in the old churchyard
   Are dancing at their will.

'A form all sapless from the tomb
   Stands where the scutcheons wave,

And trophies rattle in the wind
  O'er murdered Hilda's grave.

'In ghostly sheet a spectre stands
  Upon the midnight hill,
And wails unto the gibbous moon
  The wife of Larrendill.

'But at the crowing of the cock
  Unto their graves they'll hie:
Oh, fit night for a gentle one
  To wander forth and die!'

'I'll go with you,' said Ladye Jane,
  'Where'er you lead the way;
With you, my liege, my lord, I'll go
  From earth and time for aye.

'O Gilbert, I've longed for this hour,
  With you to be at rest;
Then roll me in that misty shroud,
  And clasp me to your breast.

'I'll slumber calm, my Red-Cross knight,
  Where'er you rest with me,
Be it by Ascalon's leaguered walls
  Or waves of Galilee.

'Oh, what reck I of Hilda's shade,
  Or, on the midnight hill,
The starlight on her blood-stained hair,
  The wife of Larrendill?

'Lead on—I'll follow—I'm your bride;
  With you, sir knight, I'll rest,
Where tons of Acre's bastion
  Are lying on your breast.

'With you, what care I for the storm,
  The raving of the sky?
O Gilbert, Gilbert, Ladye Jane
  Will go with you and die!'

He stretched his hand out, iron-gloved,
  Thro' the burning lightning's sheen,
And ne'er 'gain in this mortal world
  Was knight or ladye seen.

THE PALE BRIDE.

RADIANT the smile, and light was the step
  Of the Norland's loveliest girl,
And sweet was the bloom of the rose on her lip,
  And the wave of each careless curl;
But sharp the thorn grows, though hid by the rose:
  The maiden was false as fair,
And over my life the heyday of hope
  Set dark in the night of despair.

'I know a bride whom I yet may win,
  And to her cold lips I'll cling;
And I'll offer to her, with my gauntlet on,
  The orange flower and the ring.
I'll woo my bride 'mong the Paynim ranks,
  Far away in the Holy Land;
And I'll win my bride with belt and spur,
  And the lance in my strong right hand.

'Ho! the bastion stormed shall be my bed,
  And the sheets my dinted mail;
I'll kiss my bride, with unconquered pride,
  Through the bars of my aventayle!
I'll grimly woo with the battle-cry,
  And the corslet's blood-dimmed shine;

And a galliard I'll dance on the tented field,
   With my bride's pale hand in mine.'

And the warrior went to the Holy Land,
   And he wooed with his armour on,
And rang 'neath his tread, as he danced with his bride,
   The rampart of Ascalon.
He wooed her in steel and he wooed her in blood,
   And his bride still nearer came;
And this grim bride's fan was the catapult,
   And her girdle a burst of flame.

And warm and red was the wine she drank,
   But he loved her all the more;
She was true as steel, but the maid was not
   He had left on the Norland shore.
Wedded he lay when the day was done,
   In the burning city's breath;
And steel and fire the bride had won—
   Had won the pale bride, Death.

THE DEATH OF WALLACE.

BLACK waves the flag in young day's breath,
   Not the flag of fight, but the flag of the grave;
And the dungeon clock, with its bell of death,
   Rings for the life of the martyred brave.

Death agonies, cope with your playfellow now,
   With the manhood of Wallace of Elderslie,
With the might of a god on his proud dark brow,
   'Neath the ghastly arm of the gallows tree!

Ah! the shamble-knife for the freeman's sword,
   For the bravest heart ever throbbed in man:

The Death of Wallace.

And the sledge, and the axe, and the hangman's cord,
   For the rasping of steel in the battle van!

For the hundred fights in his own rugged land,
   The stern hero-land of the mountain and flood,
For ages compelled, with the spear in her hand,
   To water the roots of her thistle with blood!

They beheld him now on the bourne of doom,
   Who had fled when the Carron's banks he trod,
O'er the slaughter hills his plunging plume,
   Like a thunder-cloud of the wrath of God.

They beheld him now who had marched 'gainst him oft,
   With harness on shoulder and sword on the thigh,
When his battle-rent gonfalon streamed far aloft,
   And his spearmen stood round it to conquer or die.

They beheld the right arm heavy ironed and chained,
   That in far other plight they had seen oft before—
On the war-riven sod, like the lightning of God,
   It struck, and the stricken arose nevermore.

They beheld him now whose ranks, 'fore his shock,
   Were compelled in the onslaught to stagger and reel,
When the legions of England wavered and broke
   Before his wild torrent of tartan and steel.

How the naked chest throbs with the chains banded o'er,
   Heaving so brave with the life's latest breath!
O Scotland, deplore—the star-land far o'er,
   Thy Wallace has gone to the deathless in death!

And never again in the crash of the fight
   Shall a sword like to his be wielded for thee,
Or the spell of a name so splendid and bright
   Be the theme and the fire of the songs of the free!

DEATH OF EDWARD THE FIRST.

[Hearing of the coronation of Bruce at Scone, and of one or two minor successes of the Scottish arms, Edward the First, though now old and infirm, resolved to subdue, once for all, that stubborn country, the attempted conquest of which had already cost him such an expenditure of blood and treasure, and the complete subjugation of which had been the ruling ambition of his life. Collecting the armed force of his kingdom, he marched northwards, determined, as he said, to thoroughly conquer Scotland, even at the sacrifice, if need be, of reducing the whole country to a scorched and uninhabited wilderness. The infirmities of old age, added to an internal disease, and the injury received from a kick of his horse as, in soldier fashion, he lay near it during the night, so much reduced the indomitable old 'Hammer of Scotland,' that he died at Burgh-upon-Sands, near Carlisle, on his march northwards, on the 7th of July 1307, in the sixty-eighth year of his age—almost in sight of the land, the national independence of which he had determined to annihilate. It is recorded that he enjoined upon his son to lead the army into Scotland, and to carry his unburied skeleton in the front of battle till Scotland was finally crushed. In anticipation it yielded some satisfaction to the stern old soldier, that at least his bones would be present at the scene which, above all others, he had yearned to witness—the scene of Scotland's final overthrow and submission.]

THE moon shone dim in heaven,
    And the clouds, in ragged bars,
By the midnight winds were driven
    O'er the dreamy roof of stars.
Weirdly the waves of Solway
    Tossed moaning on the shore,
Wailing, in night, a dirge for him
    Who'd see the day no more.

The red star of a troubled life
    Sets not in reeling fight,
But on a silent Cumbrian heath
    It peaceful sets to night.
Solemn the mockery of Fate,
    That he whose blade flashed high
On Judah's field, by red Garonne,
    Should seek this moor to die!

Death of Edward the First.

Most resolute Plantagenet
   That ever bore the name,
Where is the might of glorious fight,
   The glare of steel and flame,
The dying groan, the wild hurrah,
   The charging battle-line,
That should have sent eternity
   A fiery soul like thine?'

True, in the darkness round you
   Are miles and miles of spear;
But there's no Graeme, no Douglas,
   There's Beauchamp and De Vere.
There's not a hostile weapon
   On all this Solway shore;
There are the daring ranks you've led,
   Which you shall lead no more!

Few are the locks and sober grey
   The iron helm hath left,
And all the cares and all the toils
   Of thy life's warp and weft;
And less of manhood's daring
   Sits on thy furrowed brow,
Less are the strength of brain and limb
   That grace thee, Edward, now.

One thing remains, undying hate,
   And fierce, for Scotland's weal,
And rancorous hatred for the edge
   Of Scotland's patriot steel:
Around thy dying bed there is
   No prayer, no saintly hymn,
But scathing gleams of wrath, which not
   The mists of death can dim!

' In Winchester, in Fonteveraud,
   Sleep heroes of my line,
But let no tomb of brass or stone
   Hallow these bones of mine.
Wherever thunder English drums,
   Where English trumpets flare,
Full shoulder high, white and erect,
   The bones of Edward bear !

' Ho, get the furnace ready,
   The caldron set thereon,
And plunge me in the seething midst,
   The moment life has gone !
And boil me till this sinewy flesh
   Fall off its osseous frame,
Then bear aloft my rattling bone
   To conquest and to fame !

' Oh, rather had I met the Scots
   Upon the trampled sod,
Than go to-night, a spirit-king,
   To meet my fathers' God :
Grim Scotland pròstrate on the field,
   With battle's thunder riven,
How joyously had Edward gone
   With his red blade to heaven !

' One wild hurrah that Scotland's down,
   Then, pale Death, ope thy door ;
His work well done, King Edward comes
   Unto thy shadowy shore.
It cannot be ; across the firth
   Lies the unconquered clime—
I die, not perfumed by her blood,
   But fragrant moorland thyme.

'O Scotland, Scotland, how I curse
　　Thy stubborn, struggling race!
All other ranks I e'er opposed
　　Have fled before my face.
And so shall yours, before my face—
　　My white face of the grave—
When meet King Edward's eyeless orbs
　　The visage of the brave!

'Wherever death stalks terrible,
　　That is the place for me,
Dash forward with the rowels deep,
　　The sword-arm swinging free—
Put lance into my fleshless hand—
　　Helm on my fleshless head—
Fight! though a thousand Wallaces
　　Should rise up from the dead!'

The monarch ceased in mortal gasp,
　　Nor ever spake again:
The Bruce, in steel from head to heel,
　　Passed 'fore his dying brain—
Blent phrenzied hatred to the Scots
　　With love for Elinore[1]—
A spasm—and the 'Hammer' fell,
　　To rust for evermore.

ELINORE.

A BALLAD OF CHIVALRIE.

'Twas high-born **Ladye** Elinore,
　　A ladye fair was she—
Her castle turrets towered full high,
Where waved the banner to the sky,
　　Down by the thundering sea.

[1] His first wife, Elinore of Castile, to whom he was deeply attached.

Her eyes were of the blue-bell's tint
  When wet with evening dew;
From 'neath the golden coronet's rim,
  Making the sheen of jewels dim,
    Her flaming tresses flew.

Her dainty glove, her tiny glove,
  Like a leaf of the leafy plane,
Often upon the warrior's lance
Had sunk in blood in death's red dance,
    The wearer's hand to gain.

. . . . .

Young Gilbert was a gallant knight,
  Of matchless arm and brain—
A braver never horse bestrode,
Nor e'er the lists of tourney trod,
Nor e'er gave up his soul to God
    Upon the battle plain.

The ladye loved her Gilbert brave,
  But ne'er her love would own,
And scornful glanced on the young knight,
As she had worn in her own right
    A monarch's starry crown.

. . . . .

'O Ladye Elinore,' he said,
  'The task you set is done,
And now let church and bridal bell
Reward my toil, 'mid carnage fell,
    That knightly laurels won.'

'I've yet one task,' the ladye said,
  'And when this task is done,
Tell me of church and bridal bell,
And rasping steel, and slaughter fell,
    And knightly laurels won.

Elinore.

' My castle wall's not broad at top,
   My castle wall is high;
Along the giddy summit ride,
With belt and spur in knightly pride,
   And win my hand or die.'

   .   .   .   .   .   .

Aloft there tramped a coal-black steed,
   And Gilbert sat thereon;
His warrior plume waved in the gale,
And, on his battle-dinted mail,
   The stars of heaven shone.

Oh, narrow is the wall at top,
   Ride wary, Gilbert brave;
High in the gloom, 'twixt earth and heaven,
Near the old banner, soiled and riven,
   Above the thundering wave!

Alone the ladye waits below,
   And looks with straining eye
At the dim form of horse and man
Moving, through her tremendous plan,
   Athwart the midnight sky.

'Tis o'er! on Elinore in tons
   The great stones tumbling go—
The task near done, the wall gave way,
Near a frail turret, worn and grey,
And dashed to death in this wild play,
The ladye, knight, and charger lay,
   Full ninety feet below.

And still, when roar the storms of night,
   And tumbles wild the sea,
A form in battle-dinted mail,
Aloft in air, 'mid fire and hail,
   From dim Eternitie,

Waves high his blade athwart the stars,
Red with the stain of olden wars,
   And spurs his phantom steed
O'er where, five hundred years ago,
He undertook, for weal or woe,
   The frantic task decreed;
And shouts 'mid ocean's wildest dash,
And o'er the thunder's loudest crash,
   'My life, my bride is won!
From the dim world of "Nevermore,"
I claim you, Ladye Elinore;
   The task you set is done!'

THE BRIDE OF STEEL.

I LOVE thee with a warrior's love,—
   My Sword, my Life, my Bride!
Dear, dear as ever knighthood bore,
Though yet no gout of battle-gore
   Thy virgin blade hath dyed!

I kiss thee, with my veins on fire!
   Grasped by my iron glove,
On the harvest-field of Death and Fame,
'Mid groan and yell, through steel and flame,
Carve out for me a laurelled name,—
   My Bride, my Life, my Love!

Take your death-bed of silk and down,
   Stale, leaden-hearted slave;
Where War's fierce roses redly bloom,
To mark the warrior's glorious tomb,
   I'd die, as die the brave!

The Bride of Steel.

From childhood I have always felt,—
    Ay, at my mother's knee,—
The bannered clouds o'er earth unfurl'd,
Eternal space and the vast world
    Not wide enough for me!

Under yon castle's feudal walls
    The battle's raging fell;
Then come with me, my Bride of Steel,—
The Dance of Death our bridal-reel;
Our music, through each rush and wheel,
    The conflict's groan and yell!

A day, an hour of high-souled life,
    Ten thousand years outweighs
Of reptile being dastards feel,
My virgin bride, my Bride of Steel,
    Whose beauty's Glory's blaze!

Is't better to crawl many years,
    Or press all life in one,
Travelling on Glory's blazoned road,
The ladder of the stars to God,
    Before with earth we've done?

I love thee, maiden, wildly, well,—
    Again I kiss thee, dear!
The grass is green, the welkin red,
The raven's shrieking for the dead:
    Our wedding-day is near!

My dinted mail shall be my shroud,
    My sexton dark the crow;
Broken and rusted, by my side
Thou'lt lie, and over us, my Bride,
    Shall Fame's red blossoms glow!

'Best of the Brave,' and 'True as Steel,'
    The minstrel song shall say;
Tuned to its most heroic key,
The harp shall ring of you and me
    Till Time's remotest day!

Who would exchange the raven's bill
    For churchyard calm and cold?—
His sword, and his last battle's clang,
The tearing of the she-wolf's fang,
The dying warrior's martyr-pang,
    For life and tons of gold?

Flushed on the bridal-bed of Death,
    My Bride of Steel, you'll lie;
And Mars, the heaven's reddest star,
Shall light the redder turf of War,
    Where we so glorious lie !

NEVER MORE.

WEIRD is the night, dark is the day,
The pride of the world sleeps in clay;
Reckless ever of life and breath,
Onward the warrior rode to death :
He, in the flush of manhood's bloom,
Mangled, rests in a far-off tomb.
O come to me from the lone dim shore !
Alas ! oh, never—never more !

Lorn I sit by your little chair,
I've a lock of your baby hair;
The very hoop you trundled round,
Unknowing of the battle-ground

Never More.

Where rams should thunder, sabres sway,
From dawn till eve one fearful day.
O speak to me as you spoke of yore!
Alas! oh, never—never more!

I see thee not, worthy thy sire,
In thy young manhood's strength and fire;
My heart turns to an earlier day,
When I would join thee at thy play,
And kiss thy smooth young childish brow—
O God! where is that forehead now?
Rise, O rise from the shroud of gore!—
Alas! oh, never—never more!

Th' embattled rock rose sheer and high
Beneath the gloomy midnight sky;
High 'mong the mist the watchfire's glow
Gleamed on the armour of the foe.
A rush—a shriek—a maddening yell,
And my son fell where thousands fell.
Speak to me—ah, the north wind's roar
Has a wild shriek of 'Never more!'

For you your sister Brenda weeps,
In the old vault your father sleeps,
And, riderless, the charger neighs
You fearless rode in former days;
And Dora of the sunny brow,
My son, my son, would wed you now.
But your bride's Death on a hostile shore,
And you'll desert her never more!

Ah, little did your mother dree,
As you lay cradled on her knee,
What hard-won laurels you should win,
What lands you were to travel in,

And 'neath the banner streaming high,
The fearful death you were to die,
And, far away from kith and kin,
The tomb you were to moulder in.
'Twixt you and me the ocean's roar
Has a wild plunge of 'Never more!'

THE CHOICE OF SIGISMUND.

[St. Augustine or Austin, according to a mediæval monkish legend, visited a place called Compton, where the lord of the manor had rendered himself notorious by his resistance to the collecting of church tithes. The cousequent incidents at Compton as narrated by Dan John, a monk of the fifteenth century, were, in all essentials, as we have recorded them in the ballad. In the seventeenth century, the Spanish poet, Calderon, based one of the most famous of his dramas on this or a similar legend.]

'TWAS in the days, the grand old days,
   Of morion and sword;
'Twas in the age, the dim old age
   Of monkish cowl and cord,
When the only light of England
   Was Ruin's fiery brand.
Where the shadow of the Abbey
   Fell darkly o'er the land,
St. Austin banned with awful ban
   The bad who would not pray,
And cursed with still more blasting curse
   The bad who would not pay.

'Depart from out this sacred fane!'
   The holy Austin cried,
'All ye profane, for whom in vain
   The blest Redeemer died!'
Out crept the guilty living
   'Fore this appalling cry,

The Choice of Sigismund.

Doomed, in their own dark consciousness,
    The deathless death to die :
They struggled out in broken file,
    Their wretched homes to find—
The ruthless roar of reddening hell
    Was in the winter wind.
They're gone ; and now the Abbey walls
    The lost and saved ones sunder.
High God! what means that whirl of smoke,
    That deafening crash of thunder?

The saints, all shaken from the walls,
    Lie shattered in the gloom,
Gusts of infernal brimstone choke
    The censer's holy fume.
The rich-stained glass is shivered,
    The symbolic Crown and Key,
And the marble babe has fallen
    From marble Mary's knee ;
And hurled as by an earthquake,
    Lies broken in the nave
The stone that had for ages lain
    Upon a baron's grave ;
While the grave itself is open,
    And rank and deep and dim,
The skulls and ribs of centuries
    Lie on its awful brim.

Blue burn the altar tapers,
    The cross glares fiery red,
And slowly from the twelve-foot grave
    Rises the sheeted dead.
The breath of ice, the stench of death,
    The Abbey fill meanwhile,
And silently the dead man glides
    Dim shuddering down the aisle.

Horrid the deep dark sockets,
   The eyes for ages gone,
The tramp of bare phalanges,
   The rattling shoulder-bone!

Horrid the dim round knee-cap,
   The pelvis strong and white;
And through each costal interstice
   The altar's candle light!
Black Ulric was a gruesome wight
   When living men amid,
But—on this yawning chancel floor—
   O God!—to meet him dead!

But still St. Austin pleaded,
   Unscared, with stedfast eye,
For needful tithes for holy church,
   The bride of Christ on high.
Then: 'Declare, O sheeted spectre,
   By all that men revere,
What mandate from the other world,
   What errand brought thee here?
I see!—Thy hard, unhallowed hand
   The tithes refused to pay?'
A gloom fell o'er the eyeless skull,
   The spectre nodded, 'Yea.'

'Where is the priest,' St. Austin said,
   'Who ne'er received thy dole,
And hurled the thunders of the church
   Upon thy wretched soul?'

Slowly uprose the fleshless arm,
   With rusted mail thereon;
Slowly the falling shroud revealed
   The damp and porous bone;

The Choice of Sigismund.

Slowly the spectral finger,
   With its ring of ruddy gold,
Pointed to a lettered tablet
   In the chancel dim and old.

'Sigismund, thou priest of God,
   I for him will pay the dole;
Rise, and on its journey hellward
   Shrive and bless this wretched soul!
Thus spake Austin, and the tablet
   Rose from out the marble floor,
And the monk of olden ages
   In the chancel stood once more.
He crossed his brow with holy water,
   Murmured o'er a Latin prayer,
And the baron, blest and shriven,
   Melted into empty air.

'Sigismund,' said holy Austin,
   'Centuries three thou now hast lain,
Dust the blood-drops of thy heart,
   Dust the ganglia of thy brain.
To smell the rose, to see the sun,
   To eat the bread, to taste the wine,
Must now be boon unspeakable
   After a horrid sleep like thine.
Then see the sun and smell the rose,
   That boon by me is freely given,
I offer thee immortal life—
   I stand, the delegate of Heaven!'

'I've lived, I've died,' said Sigismund,
   'I know the world, I know the grave,
I know the creeping of the worm,
   I know the ardour of the brave;

I know the working of the brain,
   I know the skull when filled with dust,
I know the mail in battle sheen,
   I know it, red and rough with rust.
I know your love, I know your hate,
   Your weary round beneath the sky—
Ha! *now* my heart is never false,
   And my tongue cannot lie!
Your glory is a fevered dream,
   But dreamless sleep is mine;
There's *warmth*, St. Austin, in your heart,
   But there is *peace* in mine.
I know your grief, I know your joy,
   Your heartache and your toil,
Your sweltering in the midday sun,
   Your burning midnight oil.

'I know the hovels of your poor,
   The spell that's in your gold,
Your dark defeat, and victory's flush
   Upon your banner's fold.
For, Austin, ere I doffed the cowl,
   Under this floor to lie,
I'd tried all mortal but the tomb,
   All human but to die.
I seek the deep rest far below,
   For the tossing on the wave;
And I make my eternal choice,
   I choose the Grave—the Grave!'

The rising moon smiled sweet and calm
   On the oriel's ruddy pane,
And Sigismund returned to sleep,
   Never to wake again.

GLENCOE.

[The tradition runs that the hereditary bard of the tribe took his seat on a rock which overhung the place of slaughter, and poured forth a long lament over his murdered brethren and his desolate home.—LORD MACAULAY.]

WOE, alas! and death, MacIan,
    Brood o'er Leven's sombre tide,
And the spirits of your fathers
    In the borean tempests ride.
When the storm-cloud dark is swelling
    From the ever-roaring main,
And the eagle wild is yelling
    As he swoops upon the slain,—
Seem to beckon, aerial, awful,
    Dim from the eternal shore,
Their wail, like troubled ocean, groans,
    'MaeIan is no more!'

Never more, O righteous Heaven,
    When grapple Death heroic men,
Shall the slogan of MacDonald
    Wake the thunder of the glen:
Never, when the Sassenach foeman
    O'er the bourne of Time shall reel,
'Fore the storm of mingled tartan
    And the flash of Highland steel,
Shall thy great two-handed broadsword
    Crash amid the battle din,
Son of sires who fought with Fingal,
    Clove the helmets of Lochlinn;[1]
For the phantom of your father,
    Bending from the eternal shore,
Is wailing through the Hall of Cloudland
    'MacDonald is no more!'

[1] Denmark.

Glencoe.

Lo, from this dreary rock I see
    The Future's vista dim—
The clank and yell of wildest hell
    Round visions swart and grim
Pass blazing through my rending brain—
    A throne besmeared with gore—
The plunging of a troubled sea
    That gurgles, 'Never more!'—
A shriek that starts the shuddering moon—
    Then shimmers weirdly down
Into that red, unfathomed sea,
    The royal Head and Crown:
The bubbles rise, the murky skies
    Gleam with a starry glow;
A yell of vengeance peals above,
    And agony below:
The day has dawned, and God's right arm,
    Which strikes full sure, if slow,
Has, on the mighty ones of earth,
    Avenged thy wrongs, Glencoe!
But coldly lies the moonlit snow
    On his haffets thin and hoar:
The storm wails o'er the mountain crags,
    'MacDonald is no more!'

Wave your claymores, wail the coronach,[1]
    Fill the dredgie[2] to the brim;
Far along the unborn ages
    I behold the annals dim,
See the blood of the MaeIan
    Reek up from the trampled sod,
And descend upon Glen Lyon
    Like the thunderbolt of God,
And the White Rose of the Stewart
    In its summer beauty glow

---

[1] Dirge.   [2] The cup at the funeral feast.

Glencoè. 65

'Mid the terrific grandeur
   Of the Valley of Glencoe!
But O hon, O rie! and O hon, O rie!
   Through Death's remorseless door
He's gone, our father and our friend,
   'MacDonald is no more!'

Silent now the 'Vale of Weeping'[1]
   Lies, a gaunt and frozen tomb,
And the pall of desolation
   Falls on the tremendous gloom.
Dark the mountains of Glencoe
   Lift their rock arms to the sky,
They invoke the God of Vengeance,
   They invoke the Sleepless Eye,
While the snowflakes, cold and silent,
   Grizzle o'er the mountain's head,
Shrouding father, babe, and mother
   In the Valley of the Dead;
And the shades of the MacDonalds
   Wail from off the eternal shore,
In horror at this damnèd deed,
   'MacIan is no more!'

Beneath, the slaughtered mother lies,
   With her baby on her breast;
There, torn with shot, the husband's laid
   In everlasting rest;
There, manhood's strength is levelled by
   The hired assassin's blow;
The wild wind waves your hair in death,
   O maidens of Glencoe.
From the black rocks, with heather fringed,
   When days are warm and long,

---

[1] Glencoe is the Gaelic for *Vale of Weeping*.

The fragrant breeze shall bear no more
 The lilting of your song.
'Tis blighted by the murderer's knife,
 Your beauty and your bloom,
Your merry prattle's hushed in death,
 Your laughter in the tomb:
You had your love, your trysting tree,
 Your *one* o'er all beside,
Your visions of a bridal ring,
 And you a happy bride;
But ruthless o'er the fair and brave
 There rolled Destruction's flood,
And the bridal bed's a dismal grave,
 The bridal favour's blood.
The snow shall melt, the heather flush,
 Beneath the summer rain,
But ah! the valley's maiden flowers
 Shall never bloom again.

He comes, your bard, to meet you,
 His clan who've gone before;
For earth is dark and desolate,—
 'MacDonald is no more!'

CULLODEN.

'DARK CULLODEN,' sang the Harper,
 On Mac Dhui's awful brow,
'Never, never has the Northland
 Seen a deadlier field than thou:
Never yet the rose of battle
 Ranker grew with purple bloom,
When the tartan'd sons of heroes
 Cleft their pathway to the tomb.

'Lo, I see the bolt of thunder
  Burst the future's misty veil—
Scattered o'er thy moor, Culloden,
  All the glory of the Gael;
There they lie, our sons, our heroes,
  Like sea-wreck by the reeling wave,
And thy brackens, wild Culloden,
  Stream above the slaughtered brave;
And their life-tide curdles darkly
  In the crystal of your rills:
Yelling, hear the Highland eagle
  Swooping downwards from the hills;
He comes to tear thy heart, Mackenzie,
  Cloven with the Saxon steel,
He screams o'er his wild carnival,
  The clansmen of Lochiel!

'Drumossie moor,[1] Drumossie moor,
  Thy dreary waste for aye
Shall remain a mournful record
  Of our nation's darkest day,
And mournfully—oh, mournfully,
  Down through the mist of years,
Of the last and awful grapple
  Of the Scottish Cavaliers!—
When the standard of Glenfinlas
  Riven fell to rise no more,
And the White Rose of the Stewart
  Sank amid the battle roar,
Drooped beneath the Lion-Banner,
  Never more to flush and bloom,
Scathed upon the moors of Albyn
  By the levin bolt of doom,

---

[1] The Highlanders still refer to the fatal engagement which is the subject of this piece as the *Battle of Drumossie Moor.*

Buried 'mong the wrecks of battle
   With the broken Highland blade,
Fierce death-locked in the hero's hand
   Who wore the White Cockade.

'Till the end of time the ocean
   Shall thunder on the shore,
But our grand old Scottish Highlands
   Is the Highlands never more!
The gloom of desolation wraps
   The mountain and the vale,
And the wild hare brings forth her young
   On the hearth-stone of the Gael.
No more the clans the claymore grasp
   And don the White Cockade,
No more, sweet as her native heath,
   Shall bloom the Highland maid;
No more shall dirk and target rasp
   Against the Saxon spear,
And the age must come shall barter
   A clansman for a deer;
And the laughing girl of Selma
   Must beat her naked breast,
She must, weeping, find a home
   'Mong the forests of the West,
That the dear spot where she was born
   May be a coney's nest,
That the venal Sassenach weaver
   May hunt upon the grave,
And desecrate the mountain shore
   That heroes died to save!
Down to Saxon shops and shuttles
   Can ne'er descend our pride,
For us it yet remains to die
   As our fathers still have died,

Culloden.

To seek 'mid battle's tempest,
   And the crash of sword and spear,
Six feet by three of cold red earth
   For the Scottish Cavalier!

'The records of the world shall note
   How, torn with shot and shell,
In the vortex of Death's hurricane
   The Highland soldier fell;
How heroes from the braes of Mar
   And wild Breadalbane came,
And how the Athole tartan dashed
   Through withering walls of flame.
Some far-off cairn of stones shall mark
   Where perished Grant the brave,
And where the storm of cannon-shot
   Dug leal Macdonald's grave;
Where Ross lay on his shivered blade,
   Exultant in his doom,
And down his life-earned handful bore
   Of laurels to the tomb;
And the grey cairn shall glorious mark,
   In the grapple of the fray,
Where on a holocaust of dead
   The Red Macgregor lay!

'May God help thee, Charlie Stewart,
   Low is the White Cockade;
God protect our aged clansmen,
   And the Highland wife and maid;
God be with the brogue and sporran,
   God be with the Highland blade!
Our fortune's low—our hearts are high—
   A ringing Highland cheer,
Six feet by three of deep red grave
   For the Scottish Cavalier!'

CHIVALRY.

They knelt 'fore the altar's gilded rail,
   The beautiful and the brave,
In the dim old abbey down in the vale,
   O'er high-born dust in the grave.

And martyr holy and tortured saint
   Were limned on the glorious pane,
And the sunbeams threw on the carvings quaint
   A golden and crimson stain.

And the organ peal shook the dead in their grave,
   And the incense smoke died away
Down the dim-lit chancel and solemn nave,
   Where the dead in their marble lay.

The orange wreath in the morning's breath,
   And the warrior's nodding plume,
In the hoary cloister smiled at Death,
   And the warp and the weft of Doom.

And the noblest blood in the land was there—
   The chivalrous sword and mail;
And the naked breasts of the Norman fair
   Throbbed around that altar's rail.

And the father leant on his battle brand,
   And the mother dropped a tear,
And De Wilton's Edith laid her hand
   In the gauntlet of De Vere.

And the bridal ring and the muttered words,
   And the gems and the plumes of pride,
And the whispers low, and the clank of swords,
   And De Wilton's girl was a bride.

Chivalry.

Heir to wide lands, she bore him a son
   On a sweet and a silent day :
Where the breach was won, and lost and won,
   De Wilton was far away.

And he wore her glove by his mangled plume,
   And her kiss on his lip still lay,
And his blade flashed dread as the bolt of Doom
   From the morn till the noon of day.

Wherever raved wildest the storm of blades,
   And the red rain bloodiest fell,
Wherever thickest the troops of shades
   Were hurled to the realms of Hell,

De Vere's blue flag with his Edith's hair
   Waved in the reeling van,
And rose and fell, 'mid groan and yell,
   In the chaos of horse and man.

It sank at last in the hurricane
   That raged round the knights of De Vere,
And the world span round his reeling brain,
   Laid bare by a foeman's spear.

Hearts rained out blood, helms glinted fire,
   'Mid the death groan and hooray;
And knighthood's pride toiled, tugged, and died
   Where the spangled banner lay.

For Edith's hair on that broidered soy
   Lay trampled in dust and gore ;
And Rudolph had sworn to bear it with joy
   To her bower, or return no more.

He sprang with a shout from the reeling sod,
    A gash on his helmless brow,
Raised his red hand aloft to God,
    And hissed his dauntless vow:

'Ye saints,' quoth he, 'this soy's my shroud,
    Or I bear it to Edith again!'—
But, wild as the burst of the thunder-cloud,
    Or the dash of the roaring main,

The foe swept on ten thousand strong
    O'er Rudolph's wounded ten;
The forest quakes, the mountain shakes,
    'Neath the tramp of armèd men.

And vassal thralls with husky cheer
    Rush o'er the banner fair,
The blazoned scutcheon of De Vere,
    And Edith's golden hair.

Firm faced the host the glorious ten,
    For Edith, God, and Home—
Swung the angry sea of ten thousand men—
    Dashed the battle's bloody foam.

    .   .   .   .

His horse lay on the carnage-ground
    Upon that flag of woe;
His mangled vassals lay around,
    And Rudolph lay below,

'Mid battered helm and shivered lance,
    And corslet, helm, and glaive,
And all the wrecks of War's wild dance,
    When waltzing to the grave.

Chivalry.

Sighed o'er the field the young morn's breath:
   The foemen found him there,
His pale lips pressed in ghastly death
   To Edith's crimsoned hair.

They laid him down by the side of her bed,
   The monks who his body bore;
His eyes had the glare of the eyes of the dead,
   His armour was dyed in gore.

A friar essayed the ladye to cheer
   In the mournful tidings of ill;
But the faithful heart of the bride of De Vere
   Ever, for ever was still.

Though the babe still lay on the high, white breast
   That milk to its dear lips gave,—
Years laid him again on that bosom to rest,
   When he fell in the ranks of the brave.

She followed her lord to the halls of God
   Ere that sorrowful day was done;
For her lord had died on the trampled sod:
   To a corpse she had borne her son.

Now the sire and the dame and their gallant boy
   All rest 'neath the marble there,
And over them waves the banner of soy,
   With Edith's blood-stained hair.

And swords have clashed to the valiant tale,
   And the voice of the minstrel sung,
How fair were the maids, how deadly the blades,
   When the heart of the world was young!

L'ENVOI.

The oak trees dig their roots
   Down through the armour's rust,
The wild herbs send their shoots
   Down through the wild heart's dust.

But from the tomb is lit
   Our valour's altar coal,
And fire from swords illumines yet
   The beacon of our soul.

Ring o'er the world our song,
   An anthem of the Dead;
Sing of the stern and leal,
And, with the Age of Steel,
   Inspire the Age of Lead.

Just issued, cr. 8vo, 96 pp., cloth, gilt lettered, red edged, on superior paper, price 2s. 2d., post free,

ISAURE AND OTHER POEMS.

By W. STEWART ROSS (Saladin).

'Mr. Stewart Ross has the fervour of a true and natural lyrist. This quality is exhibited to advantage in some of his smaller pieces, such as the Ode to Burns and the poem entitled "The Declaration of Sanquhar."'—*Scotsman.*

'Mr. Stewart Ross, as we before have had occasion to say . . . has decided poetic ability, and his muse seems to inspire him with a certain fantastic and weird imagery which may remind his American readers of Edgar Allan Poe—not in its rhythm or subjects, but in its passionate utterances and romantic exaggeration.'—*The Open Court* (Chicago).

'"Isaure" is pathetically and touchingly told; a story of intense passion, in the telling of which the author at times rises beyond himself and shows us of what he is capable.'—*Wakefield Herald.*

'The whole twenty-one poems are cultured, fresh, fragrant, thoughtful. . . . Every verse reveals the thinker, observer, reformer. . . . Every page glows with passion and throbs with life.'—*Oldham Chronicle.*

'In most of the poems will be found a vein of true inspiration, ringing music, deep feeling, fine thoughts, grace of utterance, and real pathos. There are here both strength and originality.'—*Oxford Times.*

'Mr. Stewart Ross possesses the genuine poetic faculty, and much of what he has written will assert its claim to more than ephemeral existence.'—*Northern Ensign.*

'Mr. Stewart Ross has already shown in his "Lays of Romance and Chivalry" that he is not only a poet, but a scholar and a thinker. And some of the effusions in the present volume maintain his reputation, for there runs through them a genuine vein of poetic inspiration. The thoughts are fine and are expressed in powerful language. He has, throughout, the enthusiasm of a genuine lyrist.'—*Perthshire Advertiser.*

'Mr. Stewart Ross is a poet of no mean capacity. There is something original in every one of his effusions, which contain many sublime touches as well as many pathetic scenes. There is something horribly tragic in his descriptive poem, "Leonore: A Lay of Dipsomania."'—*Yorkshire Gazette.*

'The poems are characterized by grace and pathos, and this further contribution of Mr. Stewart Ross's is calculated to greatly enhance his reputation.'—*Sussex Daily News.*

'Some of the poems are very beautiful, others fearful in their intensity and passion, others grand in their majesty of conception.'—*Workington Free Press.*

'Poetic effects . . . marked by a vigour of handling, they lilt along so rapidly that the reader's attention is irresistibly fixed upon the subject and the picturesqueness of its surroundings.'—*Somerset Herald.*

'Mr. Ross has both oratorical fervour and poetic taste. He possesses, too, a wide range of thought which enables him to treat various subjects in various styles, both as regards form and conception. Perhaps he is most successful in his verses on "Mabel," into which he infuses a healthy passion, and through the whole of which he sustains his character well.'—*Fifeshire Journal.*

'Can play upon the human heart as upon a harp. . . . The weird imagery, the mad passion, the hot rush of emotions, carry the reader away into the realm of dreams.'—*Northampton Guardian.*

ISAURE AND OTHER POEMS—(*continued.*)

'Mr. Stewart Ross is a man of versatile talent, and his verses show that he has the literary faculty highly cultivated. There is something wild and weird about them.'—*Truthseeker* (New York).

'A most interesting and able little volume, largely touched with the fire divine.'—*Weekly Dispatch*.

'"Isaure and Other Poems" are inspired by an imagination so vivid and strenuous, and so unrestrained by common intelligence, that they are really not safe to read suddenly in large instalments.'—*Pall Mall Gazette*.

'Whatever subject she (the Poet's Muse) touches upon, she usually expresses herself sweetly and gracefully, sometimes with a fine, flowing, forceful sweep of vigorous language.'—*Perthshire Constitutional*.

'Some of the passages are exceedingly powerful; and, as a whole, "Isaure" must be set down as one of the author's greatest poems.'—*Dumfries Standard*.

Price in wrapper, superior paper, 1s., post free 1s. 2d.; or cloth, gilt lettered, red edges, 2s., post free 2s. 2d.,

LAYS OF ROMANCE AND CHIVALRY.

By W. STEWART ROSS (SALADIN).

'Some of these effusions are of a very remarkable character, and indicate that Mr. Ross has a genuine vein of poetic inspiration.'—*Daily Telegraph*.

'Mr. Stewart Ross shows great power of dramatic expression.... The work will be welcomed by all who can appreciate poetic energy applied to the interesting and thrilling incidents of the earlier and more romantic periods of history.'—*Aberdeen Journal*.

'Many of the poems are characterized by a spirit and ringing martial vigour that stirs the blood.'—*Daily Chronicle*.

'A book of romantic, historic verse, aglow in every page with the energy of a true and high poetic genius.'—*Glasgow Weekly Mail*.

'The poems contain many fine thoughts, expressed in powerful language.'—*Newcastle Weekly Chronicle*.

'The author gives ample proof of his varied talents, and has no small share of the minstrel's magic power.'—*Aberdeen Free Press*.

'There is much that is excellent in the work.... Mr. Ross is apparently a scholar, and might make a success in some other walk in literature.'—*Liverpool Daily Post*.

'Mr. Ross is a poet of undoubted power.'—*Hull Miscellany*.

'The poems are characterized now by vigour, now by grace, and now by pathos.'—*Nottingham Guardian*.

'Mr. Stewart Ross is not only a poet, he is a scholar and a thinker.'—*South London Press*.

'The language is chaste, vigorous, and thrilling; the thoughts and figures beautiful, impressive, and elevating.'—*Bacup Times*.

'We have no hesitation, indeed, in saying that there is a true poet's fervour, a genuine originality of manner, and much fineness and richness of expression in these productions.'—*Newcastle Daily Journal*.

'The "Lays" are of great poetic merit.'—*Wakefield Free Press*.

'As to the success with which Mr. Stewart Ross has hit on the salient points of the various incidents there can be no two opinions; while there is an easy, bold swing in most of the poems which will certainly help to make them popular.'—*Brighton Herald*.

UNIVERSITY OF CALIFORNIA LIBRARY
Los Angeles
This book is DUE on the last date stamped below.

Form L9–32m-8,'57(C8680s4)444